Alfred Sereno Hudson

Fireside Hymns

Alfred Sereno Hudson

Fireside Hymns

ISBN/EAN: 9783337256975

Printed in Europe, USA, Canada, Australia, Japan

Cover: Foto ©Thomas Meinert / pixelio.de

More available books at **www.hansebooks.com**

FIRESIDE HYMNS.

BY

ALFRED SERENO HUDSON.

AYER, MASS:

PRINTED BY WM. M. SARGENT.

1888.

CONTENTS.

Contents.

FIRESIDE HYMNS.

EVENTIDE.

When slowly sinks the setting sun,
  And soft its radiance melts away,
Ere darkness sits upon the throne,
  And holds supreme its dusky sway,

Then moments come of mellow light,
  Of hallowed, peaceful, sacred calm,
With influence pure, and blest, and bright
  As hymnal sweet, or soothing psalm.

'Tis then the soul in holy thought
  Goes out to hours and scenes gone by,
And in communion sweet is brought
  With memories, that are slow to die.

As twilight's deepening shadows glow,
  The echoes of far distant years
Are heard, as voices soft and low,
  Breathed gently to our listening ears.

7

Eventide.

The absent ones, those gone before
    In fond remembrance come to mind :
That which we cherish or deplore,
    In that still hour we yet may find.

And yet there lingers o'er our heads
    A strengthening influence, sweet and blest,
That benediction like imparts
    A blessing, ere we sink to rest.

May we so live that when at length
    Life's twilight hour to us shall come,
Sweet peace and blessedness and strength
    May fit us for our spirit home.

THE OLDEN TIMES.

I.

What have the years in their flight left behind?
Ah, many a treasure we now seldom find!
Though we search for them long, and with diligent care,
There were joys in the past now exceedingly rare;
The fire-place no longer burns bright as of yore,
Sending out its bright beams on the old kitchen floor,
With its back log all glowing as snugly it lay
Against the huge chimney, mid warm ashes gray,
The ancient brick oven is closed from our gaze,
Where were baked the brown loaves of rich, golden maize,
And the beans, and "pan dowdy," and nice pumpkin pie
That so suited our taste and delighted our eye.
  They are gone, nearly gone,
   With the years that are fled,
  They lived in the past,
   But are now almost dead.

9

II.

What have the years in their flight left behind?
Ah, many a treasure we now seldom find!
The "beaufet" that once so smilingly stood
With its three-cornered shelves of unpainted wood;
The quaint pewter platters, substantial and bright;
The candle of tallow, so smooth and so white;
The hard oaken floor, that was scoured with such care;
The garret, a storehouse of relics most rare:
The old-fashioned clock with its bell note so clear,
And whose pendulum tick we could easily hear.
    They are gone, nearly gone,
      With the years that are fled,
    They lived in the past,
      But are now almost dead.

III.

What have the years in their flight left behind?
Ah, many a treasure we now seldom find!
The plain simple dress, and the old-fashioned ways,
The "raisings," the "huskings" of those early days
The "apple bees," "training days," breaking out roads,
The turnpikes, the toll gates, the stages, the loads
Of rich country produce that was carried to town
By the farmer, whose custom it was to "go down,"
The old fashioned winters, the mild early spring,
With snowdrifts and sunbeams, which these used to bring.

They are gone, nearly gone
With the years that are fled,
They lived in the past,
But are now almost dead.

IV.

What have the years in their flight left behind?
Ah, many a treasure we now seldom find!
The old district school with its three months a year,
And little red school house with benches so queer,
Where to cipher, to read, to parse, and to write,
Were deemed wholy sufficient to educate quite ;
The singing school also has passed out of date,
And the fugue tune and fiddle have shared the same fate,
As these were made use of in country church choir
Or on special occasions, by the sitting room fire.
They are gone, nearly gone,
With the years that are fled,
They lived in the past,
But are now almost dead.

V.

Thus have the years in their flight left behind
The old fashioned things that are now hard to find ;
We may search for them long and with diligent care,
And if we find them at all, 'tis exceedingly rare ;
But thanks to kind Providence, blessings quite new
Have sprung up about us, which if we should review,

11

Would take up more space than to these here belong,
So before we begin, we will finish our song,
And declare that the past we would not revive,
Nor exchange its dead treasures for those now alive.

IMMORTALITY.

The tree its leafy covering casts
Upon the chilling autumn blasts,
And wintry snows on grass and grain
Lie heavy ere spring comes again;
Yet life goes on, though tree and herb
The frost's cold fingers thus disturb;
And spring's warm breeze and genial showers
Will bring once more the leaves and flowers.
So mortal man may droop and die,
And tree like lay his garments by,
And on his turf grown grave may rise
The wintry drift, that long there lies;
Yet upward has the spirit sped,
It has but flown, it is not dead;
And better garments, brighter bloom
Are his, beyond earth's wintry gloom.

WATCHING AND WAITING.

Along the Adriatic's strand,
  The fisher leaves the shore at morn,
And far away from home and land,
  Through all the day in toil is gone.

As evening shadows dusky creep,
  And starlit night approaches near,
The fisher wives draw near the beach
  To welcome back their husbands dear.

And if perchance the hour is late,
  They stand expectant on the shore,
And sing a song as there they wait,
  That sounds above the breakers' roar.

The murmuring music gently goes
  Far out upon the waters drear,
The loved one listens as he rows,
  The dear, familiar voice to hear.

13

Watching and Waiting.

Soon borne upon the blast there come
    That well known melody and voice,
That say the wanderer nears his home,
    And soon with fond ones will rejoice.

So souls that on the sea of life
    Go out at morn, and through the day
Engage in toil, and storm, and strife,
    And seek at eve the quiet bay,

May comfort take, that when at length
    The weary voyage is almost o'er,
And faint the heart and small the strength,
    To bring them to the shining shore.

A Heavenly friend, they then may hear
    With words of holy comfort blest,
Assuring them that they draw near
    A place of peace, a home of rest.

GOING FOR THE COWS.

When hill and forest cast their lengthened shades,
And setting day in golden radiance fades,
Then come the distant echoes soft and low,
Oft heard in childhood, Co! Co! Co!
As come the words, we follow on in thought,
Until we to the pasture bars are brought;
There we behold the merry whistling boy,
With bare brown feet, and heart brimful of joy.
We pause and wait, as at the bars he stops,
And calls the cattle ere the bars he drops.
The Co! Co! Co! again sounds long and clear,
Until the farthest of the herd draws near.
Then cracks he loud his whip of leathern string,
And shouts in tones that make the woodland ring;
But scarcely has the journey home begun,
Before the youthful drover seeks for fun.
A berry bush beside the road is passed,
And on it quickly his keen eyes are cast,
Beside it busily he makes a stay,
Until he takes the ripened fruit away.
Next he ascends a tree to search a nest
Where several little fledgelings snugly rest.
Soon he draws near a stream, and up he rolls
The bottom of his pants, and in he strolls;
With hat of straw that serves a ready dish,

He scoops an easy prey, the little fish.
The bridge is reached, and there he stops to see
How large a pickerel in sight may be.
Soon comes he to the pool where sit the frogs
On muddy margin, or on rocks or logs,
These he attends to with a stick or stone,
That rashly from his hand is quickly thrown.
A woodchuck's hole in clover field is sought,
To see if yet the animal is caught.
He next at schoolmate's leisurely holds up,
To see his bantams, or his setter pup ;
And soon a serpent crawls across his path,
Exciting much the little urchin's wrath ;
Quickly the stones are showered in bush or brake
To cripple if he can the venturous snake.
Then on he goes past apple orchard near,
Where hang the "side hills" to his taste so dear ;
These cared for he again plods on,
Until a rustling comes from bush beyond ;
Within the brush-wood thick he stops to see
What such strange noise in such a place might be.
This new, important task concluded, now
He looks about in search of hindmost cow ;
But none are seen, for all are gone
Through broken rail in search of neighbor's corn.
A voice is heard, that starts the loitering youth,
And flashes full the disagreeable truth,
That through his negligence the raid was made,

And therefore on his back may stripes be laid.
Anew in roadway he reforms the line,
And starts again for home his herd of kine ;
But soon a schoolmate met, he stops to trade
A leathern string for popgun he last made.
The bargain ended, off the traders go
The new made trade, the other boys to show.
But now the setting sun is sinking fast,
The lengthened shadows dark around are cast ;
The waiting farmer leans on barn yard gate,
And wonders why it is the cows are late ;
But lo ! they come, the late boy at their heels,
While flush of conscious guilt he plainly feels,
"What made you late?" the wondering farmer cries,
As lurking guilt about the boy he spies.
The urchin cries, to stop the rising wrath,
"They sometimes stopped to feed along the path."
"Stopped, did they?" "Yes." "Who let them stop but you?
Such negligence as this you yet will rue ;
Go get the milk pails, feed the horse, quick ! start !
For mischief such as this, you yet shall smart,
And when you've done the chores, then go to bed.
Stop ! not a word ! a plenty has been said."
A moment now and all the wrath is past,
Tho' late the cows, the anger did not last.
The murmuring stream of milk into the pail
Was soothing as the note of nightingale.

Going for the Cows.

The cows slow chew the cud of stolen corn,
And all is peaceful till the coming morn,
When bright and early starts the train again,
To pass once more along the pasture lane,
And feed till evening, when the boy will go,
And shout once more, Co! Co! Co! Co! Co! Co!

THE BROKEN HOUSEHOLD.

They are gone, the scenes of those distant days,
  With life's merry morning they soon sped by;
Yet they linger in memory as sunset rays
  Are reflected in beauty on evening sky.

The home that once sheltered that household band,
  Was long since demolished from roof to sill,
Not a hearthstone escaped the destroying hand,
  The site of the homestead to point out still.

And they too are scattered who once drew near
  The fireside, as evening its mantle spread;
The circle is broken, the loved and dear
  Have joined the ranks of the silent dead.

The Broken Household.

The first, a fond mother passed over the tide,
  And we wept at the sound of the boatman's oar,
As it wafted her out on the river wide,
  And we knew we should kiss her pale lips no more.

Another was summoned, a father dear,
  Who had lovingly cared for that household band,
And our souls were sad as again drew near
  The boat, that would take him to far off-land.

A brother was next to pass from our sight,
  And narrow the circle more and more,
And again came the shadows of sorrow's night,
  As he too embarked for the golden shore.

Thus one by one they have broken away,
  The fond, loved links of that golden chain,
And been taken to realms of endless day,
  Until only two in this life remain.

But somehow we feel that that household dear
  In another home will sometime be found,
Where the boatman's oar we no more shall hear,
  And friendship unbroken will there abound.

So waiting, we sometimes sit and think
  Of what we have seen, and yet may see,
And trust, that when gathered beyond life's brink,
  We a happy household once more shall be.

A DAY AT "NOBSCOT."

(A high hill in Sudbury, Mass., not far from the famo.. "Wayside Inn.")

While yet the dew drops of the sparkling morn
Are glittering brightly on the grass and corn,
Then start the merry youth for "Nobscot Hill,"
With huckle-berries sweet their pails to fill.
The way tho' long they little think about,
But make the woodland ring with mirthful shout.
At times by spreading tree a halt is made,
When rest is taken in the cooling shade ;
Then up they start, and tramp along again,
Till soon they leave the highway on the plain,
And upward climb the steep and rugged hill,
With sprightly step and animation still.
A-while they climb, but soon the ascent is made,
And on the grass each weary form is laid.
A little laugh and talk, and then at length
Come back anew their courage and their strength.
Now for the berries beautiful and black,
Of which around there surely is no lack.
The hillside teems with berry bushes low,
On which rich clusters of the ripe fruit grow.
The pickers, tireless, seize the tempting prize,
Which in such rich profusion round them lies.
So toil they on till dinner time draws near,
When pause they, and to shady place repair

A Day at "Nobscot."

Beneath a tree with leafy branches spread,
Which screens them from the noontide sun o'erhead,
And take the store of lunch, and sit and share
The luxury of plain and home-made fare.
One from the company goes forth to bring
A cooling draught from yonder sparkling spring,
And all outstretched upon the grass repose,
And laugh and talk, as swift the "nooning" goes.
The noon hour past, once more the pickers start,
With strengthened limbs and still courageous heart,
To finish up the task that's yet undone,
Before they take the time for further fun.
Nimbly their fingers fly, and soon one hails,
" Ho boys! I've got mine full, how 'bout your pails?"
The dearest object of the berry band
He singles out, to lend a helping hand ;
And soon another fills his basket quite,
And by his work another's work makes light.
Thus toil they on with perseverance, till
Each picker does his berry basket fill,
And all rejoice at work so early done,
Since now their sport may early be begun.
"Lets go to top of Nobscot!" one cries out,
With merry laughing ring about his shout,
Then all fall in, and without thought of stop,
They soon are on the very "tip most top."
Now lo! what scenery stretches far and wide,

Extending mile on mile on every side.
A score of villages, reposing lie
In restful beauty to the admiring eye,
A hundred smiling hamlets snugly stand,
Like bright spots dotted thick on either hand.
Far to the east the gilded state house dome
Is seen, as thither-ward the eyes may roam.
Beyond South Sudbury, stands old Goodman's hill,
Where Karto lived, who owned the town until
The English purchased from him five miles square,
And paid ten pounds, a bargain somewhat rare.
This side, close at the foot of Green Hill, lies
The cemetery, where is seen to rise
The monument, that marks brave Wadsworth's grave,
Who gave his life his countrymen to save
In Philip's war, when he with comrades stout
Marched into Sudbury, and were hemmed about
By hundreds of the wild, ferocious foe,
With whom they fought until by them laid low.
A mile from Nobscot, and quite near the road,
Once stood the garrison where Brown abode,
Its brick lined walls well served a safe retreat
From savage foe, with swift pursuing feet.
A little nearer, on a shelf of land,
A Small Pox Hospital was known to stand;
The graves of victims there lie side by side,
Who of the dread scourge in the old time died.
Beyond the gentle slope of northern brow,

Brave General Nixon's farm may be seen now;
From there he went at early morn with speed
His company of minute men to lead
To Concord fight, and there the British show
That Sudbury troops were no inferior foe.
Beyond this spot, a half a mile or less,
As we should judge upon a Yankee guess,
Beside the county road, stands snug and low,
The Old How Tavern, "Wayside Inn" called now,
There stands the mansion, so set forth in rhyme,
But the "Red Horse Tavern" of the olden time,
Where stopped the traveller, and team, and stage,
That now are relics of a former age.
Here was the Landlord, jocund in his talk,
Stately in form and dignified in walk,
Squire Lyman, whom we saw at district school,
Who led the old church choir, and sung by rule;
The same who rode in quaint, old-fashioned chaise,
A sight familiar in our childhood days.
Thus objects rare, in beauty are displayed,
As far and near, the country is arrayed
With forest green, and gay as at the time
When nature's objects, all are in their prime.
But now the sound of those far distant bells,
The passing hour, by their sweet music tells.
And see, the sinking sun is getting low,
And longer by the woods the shadows grow;

And hark! the mutterings in the distant west
From clouds that on the far horizon rest,
Betoken plainly, that a storm may come,
Before the berry pickers reach their home.
The party start to make a quick descent,
And all on making haste are now intent;
The stronger help the weak, the fast the slow,
And thus in close rank, down the hill they go.
But stop! on blackberry vine one makes a trip!
And down he goes, and out his berries tip.
Then all hold up, and lend their friendly aid,
And soon again, brim full the pail is made.
Again they start, and fast they onward speed.
For to make haste, they more and more have need.
The dark cloud rises high and higher still,
Ere yet they are a half mile from the hill.
But perseverance yet may win the day,
And so the little party trudge away.
At length they reach the highway on the plain,
And yet there comes no pattering sound of rain.
The bridge is passed, South Sudbury now is near,
And far to westward, now the rain they hear,
Loud roars the thunder, quick the lightnings flash,
As in the snug house, swift the party dash.
All now are safe, they dread the storm no more,
But sit and hear the deafening tempest roar,
While bowl of bread and milk and berries sweet
They eat, and talk, and rest their little feet,

Till all the story told, by mother led,
The train starts off, and soon is snug in bed ;
Where lulled by patter of the summer rain,
They sleep and dream of berrying again.

MYSTERY.

Breaking sadly on the sea sand,
  Comes the moaning wave from far,
Bearing sometimes on its bosom
  Piece of wreck or broken spar.

Whence it came, or what its story,
  What it means, or how 'twas sent,
How long tossed on ocean hoary,
  In strange mystery all are blent.

But we know it means a something,
  Tells it of some distant land,
Whence has sailed a ship in beauty,
  Fashioned by a master hand.

Fragment of it, though it may be,
  Long in clustering seeweed draped,
Scarred and worn by many a tempest,
  Yet 'twas once in wisdom shaped.

25

So when by life's heaving ocean,
   Hopes and aspirations grand
Come cast up as gems most precious,
   Sent direct by heaven's own hand,

Tell they truly, that the Author
   Of our being here below,
Formed us in his image, perfect,
   Him to love and him to know ;

And that in the drifting surges
   Of the seething tide of sin,
We have almost lost the beauty
   We at first received from him.

THE AUTUMN EVENING.

Duskily, dreamily does the shortened day
Droop its low shadows o'er shore and bay,
Chill grows the air, till at crispy morn,
Frost sparkles on stubble and crackling corn.

Low in the air the wild water fowl flies,
Distant the echo of day sounds dies ;
Early the laborer his unfinished task leaves ;
A soft mellow haze, the light and shade weaves.

Bright glow the coals on the ash colored bricks,
Wreaths the flickering flame mid the crackling sticks,
The apples low sputter, the tea kettle sings,
The cat round the fireside lovingly clings.

Now draw near the hearthstone the family group,
Let the children be merry, a bright noisy troop,
Bring the basket of walnuts, the popcorn so white.
And let all be happy this chill, autumn night.

THE CHRISTIAN HOUSEHOLD.

Sweet is the spot where christians dwell,
    And blend in faith, their wishes dear;
Around whose altar voices swell
    With hymns of confidence and cheer.

'Tis there a hallowed peace is given,
    A respite from corroding care,
A foretaste of the joys of heaven,
    And blessings angels well might share.

When day is done and evening spreads
    Its shadows soft, through dewy air,
And twilight o'er the world has shed
    Its influence calm for all to share

27

Then round the fireside burning bright,
  The loved ones clustering, gather near,
With prayer, and praise, and spirit light,
  And feel by faith their Maker there.

And when the glimmering twilight fades,
  And deepens slowly into night,
And stars peer through the silent shades,
  And cast on earth their gentle light,

Then turns the soul to One above,
  And feels that through his grace alone
Have come the blessings we so love,
  Of strength, of friends, of christian home.

SABBATH EVENING.

When soft the Sabbath evening hour
  In holy hush, the day shall close,
And vesper hymns with soothing power
  Prepare our spirits for repose,

Then sweet it is to join in song
  With spirit voices far away,
And let our praises chime among
  The praises, sung in endless day.

Thou hallowed hour in christian home,
  For thee we speak, of thee we sing,
Far from thee may we never roam,
  And tribute to thee may we bring.

Oh, sweet communion of the blest,
  In home above, mid bliss of heaven,
Of peace like thine, rest like thy rest,
  A faint resemblance here is given.

THE BACK LOG.

The big back log of the open fire,
  How pleasant to think about,
Reminding of orchard and forest,
  With their leafy branches stout.

A hickory log, may be it is
  That reminds us of nuts in the Fall,
Of withering flowers and falling leaves,
  That so pensively we recall.

The log of an oak, it may have been,
  That stood in the green wood long,
And rattled its store of brown acorns,
  The leaves and squirrels among.

The Back Log.

An apple tree log, perhaps it is
  That sputters, and sparkles, and sings,
Reminding of fruit in the orchard,
  Which the mellow Autumn brings

A pine tree log, it may be is there,
  And the murmur once heard in its boughs
We think of, as sputters the pitch from its knots,
  And quickly to ashes it goes.

It may be the birch with its whitened bark,
  Lies daintily on the warm bricks,
And the gray moss clusters make brighter the flame
  That ascends from the crackling sticks.

Or perhaps the maple has been rolled in,
  A place for such trophy meet,
Since it reminds of its April blossoms,
  And nut brown sugar so sweet.

Perhaps 'twas a hemlock, beneath whose boughs
  The partridge with stately tread,
When springtime had flown and summer had come,
  Made snug his soft leafy bed.

Thus, whether maple or hickory, apple or birch,
  Oak, hemlock or pine, that is there,
Each, in its way, is a sweet souvenir
  Of some beauty or pleasure rare.

So as we journey the pathway of life,
    We may find wherever we go,
Some pleasure in that which we meet,
    That all other things do not know.

Each object and thing in its own time and place,
    Has an excellence wholly its own,
We may find if we will, and enjoy to our fill,
    If we take it and make it our own.

IN MEMORIAM.

(John P. Hudson, a member of the 7th Mass. Light Battery, died in the U. S. service, at Sudbury, Mass., March 7th, 1864.)

Slowly and sadly, passed the years
    Of dismal war, of civil strife,
And oft the nation sadly mourned
    The offerings rendered for its life.

The sturdy patriots went forth
    From city, village, hamlet, farm;
Unsparing was the tribute paid
    To shield our native land from harm.

In Memoriam.

And one there was who went away,
 A loved one fond, a patriot true,
He gave a brother's sad farewell,
 And joined the band of boys in blue.

Amid Virginia's swampy shades
 His camp fire gleamed, as months sped by,
Through battles stern he passed unscathed
 But reached his home at length to die.

Through weeks of watching, sad we stood
 Beside the soldier's couch of pain,
And soon we knew he never more
 Would hear his battery boom again.

The spring time came with pleasant showers,
 The hills once more, were decked with green,
Earth brought again its early flowers,
 But that dear form no more was seen.

It rests upon a sunlit spot,
 Where soft the day's departing ray
In tender radiance is cast
 Ere it in twilight fades away.

But not alone, does nature cast
 Its loving, generous offerings down,
A nation's gratitude goes out
 To those it fondly calls its own.

THE EVENING RAIN.

I.

Patter, patter, hear the rain
Beating loudly on the pane,
Telling that a storm doth reign.

II.

Wildly does the wind without
Shake the rustling tree-tops stout,
Whirl the withered leaves about.

III.

Now the roaring, crackling fire
Pile with fuel high and higher,
To it draw the household nigher.

IV.

All within the home is warm,
All within the heart is calm,
Naught is near to do us harm.

V.

God of love, for thy kind care
May we grateful tribute bear,
Long such mercies may we share.

33

DUCK HUNTING ON SUDBURY MEADOWS.

When the broad meadows soft, reposing lie
Beneath the haze of Autumn's mellow sky,
And the crisp frost of chill, October morn,
Sparkles in crystals on the ripening corn,
Then the wild water fowl begin to come
To streams and ponds, from far off northern home.
Along the river that through Sudbury town
Ranges its course through meadows broad and brown,
They sometimes tarry for awhile to feed,
Ere on their southern journey they proceed.
By day, in flocks, they wing their dusky flight
High in the air, but at approach of night
They seek some shallow pool or sheltered bay,
Where they may rest secure till break of day.
But not unnoticed do they always pass
To snug retreat, amid the meadow grass.
Traced is their course sometimes by sportsman's eye,
Who knows the reedy cove to which they fly,
His trusty gun he takes from off the hook,
And starts at once for the secluded nook.
His boat is launched from off the shelving shore,
And glides along with quiet, dipping oar.
Close to the margin of the stream he clings,
Where, mid the water brush, the black bird sings.
Now the shy musk-rat starts with sudden bound

Duck Hunting on Sudbury Meadows.

From off the bank, with harsh and splashing sound,
That makes the anxious sportsman start with fear,
Lest upward start the ducks ere he draws near.
He rows more gently, as he now detects
Through the tall grass tops, slowly gliding specks,
That tell him there the dusky squadron lie,
All snugly sheltered in the pool hard by.
And as he listens, lo! the Quack, Quack, Quack,
A noise so welcome to his ear, comes back.
In river bend his little craft he steers,
As place abreast the pool, he slowly nears.
Then with one long and calculating peep
Upon the flock, he takes his gun to creep
A little closer, but ere this he do,
His fowling piece he takes to prime anew.
When all is ready, and the distance right
To make the shot effective, then keen sight
He takes along both barrels. Lo, a flash!
And fast the deadly missiles hurrying dash.
At once the startled flock, with sudden fright,
Rise from the pool to make a hasty flight.
But stop! behold again another flash!
And yet once more the deadly missiles dash
Amid the flock, and lo! the feathers fly,
And round about, the dead and wounded lie.
Quickly the sportsman springs to seize his prize,
That flutters there before his eager eyes.

35

The wounded first are seized, then all secured,
He quickly goes to where his boat is moored.
This he draws up beside the reedy bank,
Where it is left concealed mid grasses rank.
Then he goes back and waits for further flight
Of birds, to come there ere he leaves it quite.
Round him the twilight deepens into gray,
And fast fade out the beams of ebbing day.
The wet dews, foggy, heavy, damp and chill,
The night with moisture now begin to fill.
But soon he starts! a sound comes through the air.
'Tis whistle of the wood duck's wing that's there.
Quick to his eye his fowling piece, is raised,
The trigger pulled, once more the piece has blazed.
And still again, from off the meadow land,
The fluttering bird is seized with eager hand.
Reloading, he again with listening ear,
Is all intent, still other birds to hear.
But hark! that rushing, whistling, nearing sound
Shows that a large sized flock flies near the ground.
Low lies the hunter, nearer comes the flock,
Upward he springs, and click, click goes the lock.
Whang! Bang! the charges of both barrels go,
As swoop the flock in circle small and low.
The feathers fly, and scattered here and there
A dusky form is falling through the air,
While quick with sudden start and wheel and curve,

36

Duck Hunting on Sudbury Meadows.

The unhurt fowls to other quarters move.
With loaded hand, but step and heart that's light,
The sportsman does not wait for further flight,
But starts at once to launch his waiting boat,
And soon again he finds himself afloat.
Stoutly he plies the bending, splashing oar,
That swiftly bears him towards the sought for shore.
Around the curve of river bend he speeds,
Now dark with bush or overhanging reeds.
Afar he sees the gleam of distant lamp
Beyond the meadow's mist, so dark and damp,
And on the still air now and then is heard
The whistling wing or night call of a bird.
Soon nearer comes the sounds he gladly hears,
That show him that the causeway road he nears,
A sound of travel and of rattling team,
Which rolls along the bridge that spans the stream.
Soon he has nearly reached the wished for shore,
And slacks his speed and lays aside his oar,
Takes carefully his game and gun in either hand,
Safe moors his boat and nimbly springs to land.
With brisk walk, quickly to his home he goes
To tell his story, as the game he shows.

THE BEST ROOM.

When company came it was opened,
  At other times few went in,
And the room was about as worthless
  As if it had never been.

There were books that were almost useless,
  And a stove that was kept with care,
There were lamps that were seldom lighted
  And a sofa and chairs were there.

'Twas the best room, and so it continued
  A cold, unfrequented place,
For the family would have a parlor
  To be used in exceptional case.

In the heart of humanity is there
  A room that is best of them all,
That's not opened except on occasions
  When company happens to call·

Then throw open the door that is closed,
  The shutters unbar to the light,
Make the hearth all aglow with kind actions
  And thus make its every room bright.

And fond parent, throw loosely the latch string,
  Let it dangle from every door,
And let the best room of your household
  Be kept from the children no more.

SABBATH VESPERS.

Sweet is the hour of hushed repose,
  When day's departing light is shed,
And sabbath evening soft bestows
  A gentle stillness o'er our head.

A hallowed silence fills the air,
  As incense breathed with perfume sweet,
And at the hour and place of prayer,
  The worshipers their Maker meet.

Anew the spirit turns to God,
  Anew on him, our hopes rely;
His house we feel is his abode,
  And deem his blessed presence nigh.

The tumult, toil and din of life
  Are hushed amid the holy calm;
And passion, sorrow, pain and strife
  Within it find a soothing balm.

The wounded spirit finds relief,
    A rest to careworn souls is given ;
The stricken one through clouds of grief,
    With hopeful gaze looks up to heaven.

Oh ! hour mid blessed hours of time,
    Bright are thy moments, sweet thy joys,
Reminder of that life sublime,
    Where neither sin nor grief annoys.

Still then, may this sweet vesper hour
    Of holy Sabbath's setting day,
Be bright in promise, strong in power,
    As fades its glimmering light away.

YOUTHFUL DAYS.

We would for many years be young,
    If we as long could live among
The objects which in youth were dear,
    And which we find no longer here.
But since all things must pass along,
    Which to the days of youth belong,
We, too, would move on with the rest,
    Quite satisfied that this is best.

THE OLD CLOCK.

On the sitting-room mantle, the old clock stands,
With its pale, open face, and its dark, slender hands,
And it measuredly tells with its tick loud and clear,
The lesson that all should attentively hear.

But what is the lesson that all ought to learn
From each tick, as it comes from the pendulum's turn?
'Tis this, that the time of our sojourn is short,
That not the least fraction of time can be bought,
When the grim reaper comes, to gather the sheaf
From the field, that was sown in the life he made brief.

'Tis that now is our own, and that we cannot borrow,
To make up to-day's lack, from the time of tomorrow,
That he who once loses an hour as it flies,
Can never o'er take it tho' he chase till he dies ;
For no moment comes back that has hasted away,
And none ever loiter, nor long with us stay.

Thus it is, says the clock, with its tick slow and low,
As the pendulum swings now to and now fro,
While it stands on the mantle and looks down upon all,
And thus solemnly ticks with admonishing call.

HIDDEN GEMS.

In days of childhood, I once heard
A story that my young heart stirred;
It was that in the streams around,
Were shells, in which bright pearls were found.

The meadow brooks were quickly sought,
And very soon from them was brought
Of shells, a plentiful supply,
In which the gems were said to lie.

I searched them over with great care,
To see if jewels could be there;
But disappointed, turned away,
And left the pearl case to decay.

A few days more, and as I passed
The spot whereon the shells were cast,
I looked, and lo! a jewel fair,
A tiny pearl, was really there!

The covering gross, had vanished quite,
And left the little gem in sight,
And in the place of old decay,
The precious, much sought treasure lay.

So 'tis with human gems perhaps,
There may be something which enwraps
Some noble traits, or generous deeds,
That spirit craves or nature needs.

We cast the rude encasement by,
And let it quite unnoticed lie,
But come again another day,
And bear the precious prize away.

WILD GEESE.

Chill blows the wild, November wind.
Clouds scud across the sky,
And garnered fields and leafless woods
Proclaim Thanksgiving nigh.

Yet one sign more, and then the list
Of omens is complete,
And that the distant, cackling sound
Of wild geese, high and fleet.

But, hark! the distant, well known "honk"
Comes home upon the blast.
At length, the long line heaves in sight,
The flock has come at last.

Now bring along the festive day,
With all its merry cheer,
The gray, wild geese have come and gone,
Thanksgiving day is near.

43

THE VILLAGE BURYING GROUND.

(Mount Wadsworth, South Sudbury, Mass.)

It lies upon a sunlit slope,
  Where lingering late, the sunset rays
Aslant their golden radiance cast,
  And lovingly, day longest stays.

Retired from noise of busy street,
  A calm and peaceful stillness rests
About the spot, and naught disturbs
  The scene, with hallowed memories blest.

There early does the earth present
  Its floral offerings, in the spring,
And lovingly the joyous birds,
  In soft notes, gentle carols sing.

But sweeter far than birds or flowers,
  And that which makes the place so dear,
Are recollections of the forms
  That in the dust, are slumbering there.

And sweeter yet than all, the thought
  That they whose once loved forms here rest,
Were parted from us, but to dwell
  In forms more perfect, realms more blest.

44

THE CALL OF THE BLUE JAY.

The notes of the Blue Jay (*Cyanurus cristatus*) are sometimes peculiarly pensive in Autumn. Samuels, in his "Birds of New England," states that it has an "exceedingly sweet bell like note that posseses a mournful tone like that of a far off, hamlet bell tolling a funeral dirge."

I.

Toll, toll, tinkle, toll, toll, is the call of the Jay in the Fall,
Far through the woodland is heard the sad sound,
Back comes the echo with dismal rebound,
Telling that Autumn is casting around
    Fallen and withered leaves.

II.

Toll, toll, tinkle, toll, toll, let the wild warble in sad cadence roll,
And solemnly warn, and point out the way,
That the forest leaves wither and pass to decay ;
A lesson that teaches how life flits away,
    And has its withered leaves.

III.

Toll, toll, tinkle, toll, toll, bird of wild mystery, speak to the soul,
Through the dark, leafy dell, or o'er wood covered knoll,
Still let thy strange utterance, spectre like stroll,
And mid the deep forest in Autumn time roll,
    And mingle with rustle of leaves.

IV.

Toll, toll, tinkle, toll, toll, is a call that is heard by us all ;
It comes by night or by day, is now here then away,
And though a sound that is transient, and does not long stay,
Yet listen, and hear it admonishing say,
  Withering are your leaves.

V.

Toll, toll, tinkle, toll, toll, oh, knell of existence, continue to roll,
Teach thy truth to the heart, sing thy song to the soul,
Above the roar of life's surge, let it sound like a dirge,
If by the tinkle and toll, it may often-times urge,
  That life produce more than leaves.

GOING TO BED.

Patter, patter, up the stairway, light the little footsteps speed,
Mother follows with a candle, where the darling footsteps lead.
Quickly, through the snowy night-dress, does the little head
    pop out,
"Now I'm ready for my prayers," quick, the sleepy child
    shouts out.
"Our Father" says the mother now, "go on, you know the rest,"
Soon he goes to, "now I lay me," then springs in his tiny nest.
Mother gives a kiss, and watches by the darling of her love.
Till he slumbers, then she leaves him in the care of one above.

SOMETIME.

We may not know just now,
Why hairs so silvery creep upon the brow,
But we may know sometime.

We may not know, as yet,
Why eyes so oft, with sorrow's tears are wet,
But we may know sometime.

We may not now quite trace,
The cause of wrinkled cheek, or careworn face,
But we may know sometime.

We may not know to-day,
Why joys most cherished, pass so soon away,
But we may know sometime.

Yes, sometime, silence may throw off its spell,
And silvery voices may break forth to tell
Why notes of joy and notes of solemn knell,
Within the selfsame heart, their cadence swell.

Yes, this may sometime come, then cease to grieve,
That unseen fingers are at work to weave
A covering thick, no finite thought can cleave,
But all thy mysteriess with Another leave.

HEAVEN.

*"And God shall wipe away all tears from
their eyes."*

REV. vi. 17.

I.

No toil nor tears,
No doubts nor gloomy fears,
  No drear distress
Await the ransomed band
In that eternal land
  Of love and holiness.

II.

No sobbing moan
Of grief's deep undertone
  Disturb the heart
In that celestial sphere,
Where dwells with loved ones near,
  The immortal part.

III.

There all is light;
No gloom of gathering night
  Breaks on the day;
But beams from God's bright throne
Shine and have ever shone
  With pure, unblemished ray.

IV.

No seas divide,
No mountains rise to hide
  From friends or home,
But all together there,
Like joys, like comforts share,
  And no more roam.

V.

No sickness there,
No pain for flesh to bear,
  No sad heart-ache,
Of happiness and health
In store a constant wealth
  Each may partake.

VI.

Sin is not there;
Temptation will not dare
  To vex the soul;
But pure and unmixed bliss
Of perfect holiness
  Be ours, while ages roll.

VII.

To that abode,
Blest Saviour, bring the soul,
  When life shall cease;

Oh, by thy grace may each
That blessed country reach,
Where all is peace.

RESIGNATION.

When sorrows strange and conflicts wild
  Perplex the soul and press it sore,
And oft misfortunes wave on wave,
  About us brake, around us roar,

Then with a look of humble faith,
  May we our blessed Master see,
And hear him say, "be not afraid,
  'Twas I of old who trod the sea."

A calm in conflict he can bring,
  Tumultuous passion cause to cease,
The angry billows quickly tame,
  The stormy surges soothe to peace.

His voice above the din of time
  Speaks gently to our listening ear,
A hand in succor, he extends
  To soothe each wound, to wipe each tear.

No contrite soul his mercy sought,
    And ere was empty sent away,
No wanderer ere to him was brought,
    And was not by him bade to stay.

Blest Saviour still to us reveal
    The one true source of sweet relief;
Still show thyself the blessed fount
    Of consolation in our grief.

Teach us the lesson, hard to learn,
    That never does thy love depart,
Tho' all things else may fade and change,
    And sorrow wring the stricken heart.

THE RIGHTEOUS DEAD.

When in the plan of One above,
    The life with lengthened virtue blest
Is full, and God has called in love
    The christian to a place of rest,

Let not the living sadly grieve,
    Nor long lament the spirit fled,
But fondly with the Master leave
    The loved one dear, the righteous dead.

Far, far to other realms, the soul
    Has soared in ecstacy sublime,
To dwell with Christ while ages roll,
    Beyond the taint of things of time.

The toil worn hand reposes now,
    The life of weariness is o'er,
The victor's crown is on his brow,
    His feet have touched the heavenly shore.

No more of toiling, watching, pain,
    He now has laid life's armor by ;
For him to pass away was gain,
    It was not death for him to die.

Safe in the courts of God above,
    From earthly turmoil, care and strife,
He shares within that home of love,
    The blessings of immortal life.

In truth of him it may be said,
    The blessed memory of the just
Will linger, tho' the form is laid
    To slumber in the silent dust.

NO. NOT FORGOTTON.

I.

No, not forgotten are they, friends of our early days,
Who walked with us in childhood along life's pleasant ways:
Tho' distant far, the echo of each loved, familiar voice,
Yet through fond recollection they still the heart rejoice.

II.

No, not forgotton are they, but live in acts of love,
Tho' long ago they passed from earth and found a home above;
Tho' dead, they yet are speaking, and the deeds they left behind,
Live with a silent life of love, that us to them still bind.

III.

No, not forgotton, some one perhaps may say of me,
When I have passed from mortal sight, and ceased from earth
    to be.
Some word that I have spoken, some deed that I have done,
May make me still remembered, cause thought of me to come.

IV.

Then may each word be gentle, soft spoken, pleasant, kind,
A word that I shall wish some friend may yet recall to mind;
May every act be loving, to friendship be found true,
That they receive a blessing, who may my acts review.

BEREAVEMENT.

When in sorrow, mortals languish
    O'er the loss of those they love,
And the heart that's wrung with anguish,
    Seeks its rest in God above,

Tells He of a blessed country,
    Far away in realms of light,
Where no death nor sorrows enter,
    Where there are no shades of night.

Parting words are there unspoken,
    Farewell message is not known,
Ties of friendship ne'er are broken,
    Hearts are never left alone.

Flowers whose petals there once open,
    Never close nor fade away ;
Fruits which in that sunlight ripen,
    Never fall and ne'er decay.

Then sad soul look unto Jesus,
    Thickly tho' the tear drops fall,
Lovingly he waits to cheer us,
    Bear our burden, hear our call.

Leave the loved ones he has taken,
    To the tender shepherd's care ;
He, thy heart will not long chasten,
    E're his blessing thou wilt share.

GROWING OLD.

We are growing old? Oh, say it not!
For tho' it is the common lot,
Of us it has been quite forgot.

We are growing old? do not thus say;
We feel in spirit blithe and gay,
As when in childhood's distant day,
We thought our youth would ever stay,
And only wished our years away.

We are growing old? it may be so;
The years they come, the years they go
By process that we hardly know,
As sea sand when the tide is low,
A moment and it comes in sight,
Another, it has vanished quite,
So pass the days, and speed them by;
As weaver's shuttle, swift they fly,
Nor deem we that old age draws nigh.

Thus pass the fleeting years away,
So quickly, youthful joys decay,
Thus comes the evening of the day,
So soon we sit in twilight gray.

55

THE STORMY DAY.

The wind a lonesome traveler,
　From ocean brings a storm,
From off the heaving billows
　Its moaning sound has come.

Wild murmurs, as of surges,
　Rush over hills and glades,
Sad sighing, as of dirges,
　In dismal echo fades.

But safely, snugly resting
　Beneath a shelter warm,
We listen to the tempest,
　Without one thought of harm.

A sound that soothes to soft repose,
　Comes to us nestling dry,
A calm amidst the blast that blows,
　The rain's soft lullaby.

CHURNING.

Early and bright by the rosy light,
  The farmer's wife fills up the churn,
Then calls in a boy both brisk and bright,
  The crank of the churn to turn.

He starts with vigor, the duty to do,
  And turns with a will the mill,
But soon his courage and patience too,
  Show that of churning, he has had his fill.

"A few strokes more," the good woman says,
  "For to gather the butter's begun;"
He starts up anew, and puts in the few,
  But soon finds that the work is not done.

Weary and worn, the tired boy turns
  The crank of the cream mill still,
Till the late morning hour has exhausted his power,
  Ere the churn, with the butter he fill.

At length, with his patience almost worn out,
  And with back-ache and fingers sore,
The butter has come, and he starts for home
  With a few pennies to add to his store.

Churning.

He forgets, in his love for the treasure bright,
  How trying he just thought his lot,
But in new found joy, the light hearted boy
  Thinks only of what he has got.

In turning the crank of life's greater mill,
  How often the butter comes late,
And peevish, complaining, we get out of sorts,
  And still turning we fret as we wait.

But courage my brother, the splashing is near,
  Of butter-milk in the churn,
And soon you can make the bright golden cake,
  If you continue with patience to turn.

Tho' back ache, and side ache, these are trifles quite small,
  If to blessings they quickly give way,
And there come for your pains, the much wished for gains
  That will every past trouble allay.

THE TWO PATHS.

Oft in the stilly night come scenes in dreams,
   That strike the slumberer with a strange surprise,
And waking, wonder we at what has passed
   Before the vision of our spirit eyes.

Thus was it when in dewy darkness wrapped,
   The earth was still, and few were near to hear,
There came soft sounds whose gentle echoes fell
   Upon my listening, half enchanted ear.

The scene in dream-land was a sun-lit slope,
   That peaceful lay with flowery carpet spread,
Where merry children joined in pastime sweet
   Beneath a sky of summer blue o'er head.

Awhile their mirthful, merry shout rang out,
   And naught diverted from their youthful play,
As if to them there never was a thought
   That such fond scenes would ever pass away.

But suddenly a spectacle was seen
   Beyond the play ground, and all turned to view
The scene before unnoticed, and which looked
   As something to them altogether new.

The object was a calm and soft expanse
  Of water, as of broad and peaceful stream,
Which noiseless, glided by the flowery banks,
  As bright the golden sunset on it gleamed.

All for a moment stood surprised, and gazed
  Upon that silvery surface clear and bright;
Then sped the little feet as if in haste
  To reach the spot and share in its delight.

But lo! they found as sped they toward the shore,
  A pathway had been fashioned, plain, direct,
And on each side the entrance pillars stood,
  From all mistake the traveller to protect.

A voice was also heard, as from the skies,
  Bidding them pass this entrance straight and plain,
Instructing them that there they each should pass,
  If that celestial stream they hoped to gain.

Part of the company at once went in,
  Their little footsteps pressed the better way;
But some passed round it, wishing not to go
  Where thus to enter would be to obey.

But ere the shining object they drew near,
  Afar they look, and lo! a glorious sight!
A something beautiful, majestic, grand,
  Is seen approaching o'er those waters bright.

The Two Paths.

'Twas mystic boat, that silent made its way,
    Propelled by neither wind nor tide nor oar !
And came from out the distant radiance dim,
    As if direct from Heaven's celestial shore.

In ecstasy they now draw near, and wait
    The gliding boat, to welcome to the land ;
All now alike the stream's bright bank have reached,
    And eager stand upon the glittering strand.

All now expectant hoped to be received
    Within that boat, so beautiful and bright,
And safe upon those silent waves be borne
    To place of peace, to scenes of fond delight.

But sad to say, part only stepped within,
    And those the ones who passed the chosen way,
Along the shore the others waiting stood,
    Nor for them did the boat a moment stay.

For them it was to backward trace their steps,
    And walk the pathway made so clear and plain,
That they too might be borne beyond the tide,
    When mystic skiff should touch the shore again.

The dreamer woke, with heartful joy to find
    That still to youth there is an open door,
Which by repentance may in life be found,
    And when once entered, feet will stray no more.

And sometimes now the dreamer offers still
In supplication strong, the ardent prayer,
That when on distant stream the boat is seen,
A place for every loved one may be there.

So may we each in unison rejoice
That Christ an open way has made for all;
That each may entrance find to rest and peace,
Who come obedient to his gracious call;

That sunlit sea and not a cold dark stream,
Rolls wide its glittering waves to spirit land;
That silvery may the boat and boatman be,
That come to waft us to Heaven's waiting band.

And when, at length, the far off shore we see,
And glittering boat to it is drawing near,
May there for each a place within it be,
And words of welcome fall on joyful ear.